Today

~

101 Ghazals

Today

~

101 Ghazals

Suzanne Gardinier

The Sheep Meadow Press
Riverdale-On-Hudson, New York

All inquiries and permission requests should be addressed to:

The Sheep Meadow Press
P.O. Box 1345
Riverdale-on-Hudson, NY 10471

Cover image: *American Cream, Diptych #3* by Dona Ann McAdams
Designed and typeset by The Sheep Meadow Press.
Distributed by The University Press of New England.

Printed on acid-free paper in the United States. This book meets the guidelines for permanence and durability of the Committee on Production Guidelines for Book Longevity of the Council on Library Resources.

Library of Congress Cataloging-in-Publication Data

Gardinier, Suzanne, 1961-
Today : 101 ghazals / Suzanne Gardinier.
p. cm.
Poems.
ISBN 1-931357-57-9
I. Title.
PS3557.A7114T63 2008
811'.54--dc22

2007035755

Acknowledgments

Ghazals 45, 50, and 95 first appeared in *Literary Imagination*, Vol. 9, No. 2, 2007.

Ghazal 101 first appeared in *Lumina*, 2006.

Thanks also to the President's New Venture Fund of Sarah Lawrence College for freeing some of the time in which these poems were written.

Thou art all fair, my love; there is no spot in thee.

–*Song of Songs* 4:7

Allí me dió su pecho;

Allí me enseñó ciencia muy sabrosa,

Y yo le dí de hecho

A mí sin dejar cosa;

Allí le prometí de ser su esposa.

–*Cántico Espiritual* 27

No defect canst thou see in the creation of the God of mercy;

repeat the gaze, seest thou a single flaw?

–*Koran* 67:4

Dear Shahid,

The last time I heard your voice was at your memorial, in April of 2002, in a hall of your lovers at NYU, so many I had to sit on the floor. Did I ever tell you that yours was the first ghazal I read, in manuscript, when I worked at Ben Sonnenberg's *Grand Street*: "The only language of loss left in the world is Arabic," you wrote, jostling my ignorances as you keep doing, far though you are now.

Here are 101 bent ghazals, although I hesitate to call them that, remembering your impatience with "Westerners" (your quotes via Edward Said) mangling the form. I've kept the exigencies of the couplet, and of the *radif*, and of the *makhta*, and neglected, forgive me, those of the usual number of couplets and of rhyme and strict meter. (One odd substitute: the number of couplets is always prime.) I've observed as best I could the "stringent formal disunity" you pointed out the form demands, but have occasionally permitted a little union to sneak in; maybe I've been truest to your least technical requirement: "What defines the ghazal is a constant longing." I confess I've bent sonnets as well. Whether as a result I've made matters far too easy on myself, as you might say, I leave for you to decide.

Love to you,
Suzanne

Manhattan
2005

~1~

I can hear you but I can't see you
That's your plan for me isn't it

The branch of the cherry along the path
is interrupted by blossom isn't it

Three cardinals on sand in my dream last night
Night is a lesson in thirst isn't it

Two chairs One where I sit and wait
This is your idea of love isn't it

Pruned forsythia Sprays of carbon monoxide
A Columbus Avenue dialogue isn't it

If I could put my lips to your shoulder
That's also a shirt between us isn't it

If I can't see you shall I make you up
That's a red bird stammering isn't it

~2~

Are you listening I'm whispering tonight
By the sycamores Where we do not meet

Or another room Why not It's safe this way
In your kitchen Your garden Where we do not meet

Salt garden The smell of thyme And balm
for the bees Where you're barefoot Where we do not meet

A painting without light Two Women Sleeping
Far from avenues Where we do not meet

Maybe you've forgotten Let me tell you my dream
My mirror-play My farce Where we do not meet

Your pale strong hands making semaphores
until you still them Where we do not meet

Your hair hiding its gray Your laugh your sadness
Rain and thirst Which do not meet

Here's a feast table A prayer mat An airport
A lexicon of rooms where we do not meet

Here's a dock Where we tie up what we've made
A moored salt room knocking Where we do not meet

Or a stable Where the long night rides started
Where you keep me faithful Where we do not meet

Day A path between locks Work and bed
Host to an absence Where we do not meet

Night My lips at your ear Were you sleeping
Let me here at least Where we do

Not meet The far one Her hair hiding
her secret And the whisperer Who do not meet

~3~

The moon coming up in early September
Clock replacer Telling the time

Used moon Rusty at the start of its aria
Making its own measures Telling the time

It crosses the sky like a shark Like a scythe
A current of white lava Telling the time

A match set to the warehouse of licenses
Of synchronized watches Telling the time

Over neon imitations Over unquiet ruins
The city looking down Telling the time

Oh but up Up A reckoning
on the terms of the tide marshal Telling the time

Night terms Terms to make your chest ache
if you lift your face Telling the time

Finding you by the smeared window Touching you
under your clothes Telling the time

Variations on the theme of burned scaffolds
you thought were buildings Telling the time

Variations via sweat and gin and jasmine
Scald of milk Tenderly Telling the time

Not all night Just a long arc through the sweet part
Close your eyes There it is Telling the time

Two women again No one knows them
but the breaker and enterer Telling the time

One pulling the blind One writing two letters
One to the moon Telling the time

~4~

Your eyes are still closed but they move You're dreaming
The end of the long night ride nearing Not here

Dreaming of a plane pressed to a plank
Finding the curve in the stiffness Not here

Make it wet and it bends A can of varnish
and the bend is a boat But not here

A car is burning An intersection A city
The emperor waving and smiling Not here

Here a pine made an arc made a room is salt wet
for the first time It's morning But not here

Someone beside you stirs and you hold her
Answering the night's last question Not here

In another morning she was a girl
and found where you were hiding Not here

Awake and asleep The trim skiff and the water
Here Not What language is this Here Not Here

The first time they hardly know each other
The hull and the wave But they learn But not here

The sound of it The slap and suck
of the introduction But not here

The curve of your back Your breasts forgetting
the night lessons Starting the day's But not here

Where the emperor laughs Where a car is not burning
Closer and closer Not here

Where someone sleepless kisses your eyelids
in a room made of words Not Here

~5~

Bread in your hand Two branches of grapes
in a bag that touches your wrist On the street

The baker The grocer Whose names you know
The late weekend morning greetings on the street

Tea in paper Its bitterness softened
with milk The sun in your eyes On the street

The sidewalk tree turning its split leaves gold
Not yet Not spilling gold fruit on the street

The tree that only bears fruit when it's old
Grandfather-grandson tree On the street

Tea in paper printed with messages
Lifted to your lips on the street

The lovers blinking in brightness Their hair wet
Pausing to forage for food on the street

Your brisk step Your key in your pocket Your parcel
of not wheatfield Not wine On the street

The split leaves can fall in an hour when it's time
A circle of ribbed gold fans on the street

The emperor garbling the messages
Dancing in broken glass on the street

Two women Not meeting One holding a key
One tasting the wheat and wine there On the street

~6~

In a dream In a room that doesn't exist
In an occupied city Two women dancing

The emperor's searchlight finds the room's corners
but they keep to the dark parts Two women dancing

Who's the leader Who the follower Cheek
to cheek as they say Two women dancing

How do they know where to put their feet
One leaning One yielding Two women dancing

Stalked city Or is the hunting over
Helicopters and two women dancing

Deeper than the sea sings their instructor
Someone dead teaching two women dancing

Light through the slits in the walls of the garrison
Press the closure it opens Two women dancing

To the tune of ashwind Of the guards pacing
To the tune of sirens Two women dancing

Loosened Untied Unleashed Undone
Whose are they Contraband Two women dancing

One with a ring on her left hand's third finger
One with a scar there Two women dancing

One lowering a mask of mirrors
One a mask of ink Two women dancing

~7~

On a slip of paper you find in your fingers
one dusk in the spring My name

Whenever we sit here you make me repeat it
Read from the palm of your hand My name

A scaffold An arrangement of bones the wind
moves through to make bent music My name

Trapped in the silence of icebound cordage
Buried in shallow cove clam mud My name

Scourge Cipher Gutbucket Quarry
On the lists of drunks and debtors My name

On the slip of salt fog you find yourself breathing
just as you fall asleep My name

On your lips but no Under your tongue
as you don't kiss me My name

~8~

for Edward

Now you live in the country you didn't believe in
Your death a year old Exile's home

Hot bread dipped in oil and *za'atar*
Polyglot dawn in exile's home

Thyme from far spring hills Sumac and hyssop
Lebneh on Broadway Exile's home

Yellah It's September The renegade scholars
with your name in their mouths today Exile's home

Ma'asalaama arrowmind atheist
comrade But you're still pacing exile's home

Ka'ik and cucumbers Your view of the Hudson
Of the country you did believe in Exile's home

The heaps of *za'atar* in the market stalls
of the city that doesn't exist Exile's home

Pale spices muffled in plastic on Broadway
The taunt of nearness Exile's home

A cup of pomegranate where you were born
Half there and half not there always Exile's home

Ma'asalaama But your words persist
Your humming Your fury Your cufflinks Exile's home

And this two-part invention This listener
who misses you *Shukran* Exile's home

~9~

I've lost my shoes Have you seen them
The winged ones that used to carry me

I've heard that when people die they remember
their mothers and call in the night Carry me

When my son used to say I can do it myself
he was whispering Could you carry me

When the quick rain soaks the shoulders of my shirt
it's saying Just for now Carry me

There's a tenderness around your eyes
Have enough tears said Carry me

All day in this new dream I walk on gravel
and the words you didn't whisper carry me

When my mother arrives at the end of something
it's to faint in my arms and say Carry me

I've known how to walk since before I was born
It's useless to try to carry me

What the dazzle of light says as it touches
the wave swelling Cresting Breaking Carry me

What the secrets say as they line the edges
of my eyes Your eyes Carry me

What the shoeless stammerer doesn't say
as she doesn't step into your arms Carry me

~10~

At the end of the day when you're tired come find me
Put your head in my hands Just rest

It's raining but not here In this room
we're turning the grindstone to mint Just rest

How many ways do you know to say peace
The emperor's absence These arms Just rest

Wet hibiscus bulbs on Columbus After
Beginning the winter turn toward just rest

Tomorrow the grid of orders and divisions
Not now Our two mouths make one gesture Just rest

For an hour close your accounts and your eyes
The ordinances blurring Just rest

I've forgotten to sign my letter again
The restless one Listening to your whisper Just rest

~11~

Put your finger to my lips will you
Before I say something past forgiving

Tell me where your hands have been
Tell me what you've done that's past forgiving

I know someone who's free but not here
Past touch Past memory Past forgiving

The guards in lines try to take off their flesh
and put on steel Past death Past forgiving

Your voice A clear stream over gravel Laced with trembling
A hesitation between orchards Past forgiving

Your ankles pale on the couch The day fading
Did you mean to show me what's past forgiving

The way your hips used to tell me the truth
that is not the truth and is Past forgiving

Those the guards touch strapped in ice and plastic
The faces on street posters Past forgiving

The emperor's loyal ones cheering Is this
how our children will learn what's past forgiving

A woman with a photograph Her mother's face
Which of them is past forgiving

Who's here Your trespasser Blinder of witnesses
Past purity Past famine Past forgiving

~12~

Breakfast of *lebneh* and strong Irish tea
Come join me for the colonized feast

Sit in the empty chair Sit on my lap
I know how to watch without tasting the feast

From América one ripe banana
What was your name before the guards' feast

One bolted scallion to keep away sickness
Raised from its burial Scalding feast

And milk The emperor's cows are fat
They can't tell if they're the hosts or the feast

My grandmothers from Belfast to Damascus
Their stomachs growling Serving the feast

Your dreamer here in the night made a table
Enough chairs Only just sorrow Feast

~13~

The pearl I thought I was looking for
The years I would spend all night asking

The moon dim above the imperial searchlights
Is it alive Is that what you're asking

When you circle the room with your hammer and nails
battening Are you telling or asking

Will you teach me Will you touch my ears
so I can understand what you're asking

Is it now No Wait Not yet
The question the unbroken wave keeps asking

The pearl hidden deep Smooth from rough Taut Wordless
My tongue knows all the suras of asking

The saltspray roses at the edge of the thicket
The red plums blackened What winter is asking

The emptying I thought I wanted
Did you learn this too To make feast out of asking

When she speaks in a way that isn't familiar
can she still make you laugh Can you hear what she's asking

Desire like a plummet Watch from a distance
The beautiful helpless arc of asking

Your interrogator wants to stop wanting to know
Who are you Where did you come from Just asking

~14~

When you lived by the stable what did you see
A horse's face without a bridle

Did you walk the park path made of cinders
Made for the curb and the quirt and the bridle

A wall of tack The stalled horses dreaming
a wall of apples No bit No bridle

I dreamed you wore the mask of a horse
A white horse accustomed to beach and no bridle

How many hands high Look You're unfolding
The salt wind at your temples a bridle

On the long night rides I sit behind you
or is it astride My costume our bridle

Are you riding or running Your passenger's asking
Her cheek at your neck This one night our bridle

~15~

Zukkar to *azúcar* Did an oud cross the strait
to teach a Cádiz guitar to say sweet

Too much and it tips Stand on one foot and find it
The dizziness Part fear Part sweet

The old city's name meaning enclosure
A castle wall Which side sweet

Look down from the ramparts *Carnaval*
The masked dancers teaching the stone ways sweet

Nuptials Swords Ships with cannon ports
left for the magistrates Here it's sweet

Almond and cinnamon Apricot cakes
Your teeth at my lip to temper the sweet

To gather the strength to keep near enough
The all-night lesson Succor Sweet

To be wise in it taste *Sabor y saber*
A little in my bowl Then vanished Sweet

The city's throat closed to the emperor's edicts
Bolting the gates Drunk on sweet

The line of your cheek as the color rises
Are you putting your mask on again Is it sweet

Goodbye to the flesh But one night is long
Someone's playing all the notes she knows Playing sweet

Your heel Your lip Late bent note
Your name in a dream All the ways to say sweet

The one for your clown here always motley
Cake of honey and dirt My ash dance My sweet

~16~

Do you remember what you told me
when you were sitting on my lap last night

In a chair But not any one we know yet
In a city in which we were strangers last night

The arms low enough for your knees to rest there
Strong enough to hold you last night

On my lap frontwards You forgot your costume
and I forgot to remind you last night

A splint made wet to learn to bend
The arc of your back in my hands last night

I was wearing a mask in the form of a shirt
But you undid the buttons last night

Your breasts speaking silence My tongue the translator
We had a long conversation last night

What did I think I would do with it
What I thought I could keep from you last night

What my fingers inside you made us say
Your lips against my listening last night

Who made your face Who made the chair
by a window that was our bed last night

Your listener kept hearing it City bled white
just outside our window last night

~17~

Tonight your high room is dark You're not there
Shall I tell you your new address Where you live

Behind my eyes every time I close them
Does it always ache like this where you live

Is there always a feast table short one chair
and a bottle of red I can't drink where you live

Je voudrais te dire pero imposible
Where's the book of the language of where you live

In the whorls of my ears My fingertips
The lips that used to be mine Where you live

In my chest where the fire tries to teach the rain
The fire you breathe alive Where you live

In my belly that used to settle for food
My belly that growls without you Where you live

In a woman's body In the emperor's city
laced with rebel musics Where you live

In my hips Did you know I'd just learned not to wake them
Does anyone get any sleep where you live

In the hair that says I'm grown and know better
Is this what being grown means where you live

In the heels my mother didn't hold as she dipped me
in the river without end Where you live

Are you somewhere behaving yourself tonight
Far from this gutbucket gin joint Where you live

Who's still up ransacking the changes past three
Where you joke and make hard words sweet Where you live

~18~

The road I walked to you Yours to me
Seest thou a single flaw Perfect

The razed field of subversive strawberries
and the girl eating one saved Perfect

The olive that died in its time and the one
dead in its time of harvest Perfect

How you pin your hands under your elbows
and how you touch me everywhere Perfect

The scythe that came in the winter to find me
so I could lie beside you Perfect

How you stood behind me to keep off marauders
and how you stepped aside Perfect

A woman you love who laughs at me
Another who gave me her blessing Perfect

The tears of a woman I love as the wave of you
pours into rooms we knew Perfect

My children who dream you're an edict A robber
A match set to paper rooms Perfect

The razed house Bits of plates and sheets in the rubble
Lullaby for the world we know Perfect

Design without flaw The righteous sermon
and the dancers to other music Perfect

The children disputing the avenues' titles
The gates that would not hold them Perfect

You and your templates Your faithful one jabbering
Repeat the gaze Praise to it all Perfect

~19~

Irish tea from Assam and Kericho
Did it change names crossing the border

The smallholders' plots in the rift valley highlands
Sweat becomes pleasure across the border

Two leaves and a bud One girl with a basket
as tall as she Across the border

The bushes smuggled out after partition
The divided ones calling across the border

A regiment of tea drilling over
the ghost of a forest Across the border

A terrace of pickers The ache in his neck
The cuts on her hands Across the border

The growing tips to the withering trough
Cut Torn Curled Across the border

Three shillings per kilo The smell of her tiredness
What will it sell for across the border

The auction Monday mornings in Mombasa
What leaf plus stoop means across the border

The savor of hunger Of take Of plantation
Can they taste it in Belfast Across the border

Plantation of cocoa Cinnamon Jasmine
The cost of sweet Across the border

Two Mombasa garlands A needle through
each closed blossom's tip Across the border

In an acre five hundred pounds of blossom
Is that Vishnu lifting one Or a girl Across the border

Threaded blossom opening on the neck
of the bride Of the groom Across the border

Or the spent blossoms reddened and crushed in the lawless
lovers' bed Across the border

Two leaves and a bud That dip and pivot
The ache it makes Across the border

Here's a witness Two aches One of absence
and one of partition Across the border

~20~

The gatekeeper fallen asleep The lock slipped
from the hasp and the way open when you come

The white stallion or is it a mare
who moves in the dark just before you come

Arched and held firm Lost and intent
Torn and joined Rent Beloved When you come

My voyager Vaulted Verge and tip
and tongue and lip and whisper when you come

In my mouth scraps of the song with no words
you leave trembling there when you come

At the angel's behest and mercy driven
down the throat of the tempest When you come

The parched ache at the cistern brim
The rapture of the dipper when you come

On the third circumnavigation a harbor
called Salt Taste That Greets You When You Come

Is it you or the angel wet with sweat
filling the room with God's name when you come

The paved beach and the wetness of the brook
freed from the burying ground when you come

Someone almost there Your shepherd of ache
whose stray ones are gathered again when you come

~21~

All night your breath at my neck and this rocking
Carried limp in a lion's mouth

Plush underfoot Arched vault overhead
Template of a palace A lion's mouth

Teeth but you keep them from tearing me
The long night ride in a lion's mouth

Breathing high plains and the deft leapers' heartbeats
Smeared with blood A lion's mouth

Knowing and deep How you come when I'm sleeping
Beyond the settlements A lion's mouth

Shall I show you how brave I am
My head all night in a lion's mouth

The rock of your heartbeat Your paws on my chest
Your tongue Your growling A lion's mouth

Guttering candle lit Not at the hearth
My hips pressed to a lion's mouth

Your voice that makes the bent grass tremble
In danger In darkness A lion's mouth

The chair The whip The emperor's shouting
All for the soft wet lion's mouth

Your prey still pinned open remembers
a little death A lion's mouth

~22~

Your fingers in my hair without touching me
What is it you want Playful teaser

My nipples only for hiding and children
You keep waking them Why Playful teaser

The taste of death in October evenings
Or is that the taste of life Playful teaser

Work and what's certain Let me live there
Let me die there Playful teaser

Here's your stumbler Lost in the footprints on the floor
Teach me to dance Playful teaser

~23~

The claw of a crab The sweet flesh near the elbow

I say I'll stop when I'm full but I don't

The dawn soft over dark apartments

I say I'll turn and go home but I don't

Who are you What do you want from me

I say I'll ask without smiling but I don't

The burning curry missing the mango

I say I'll forget the sweet but I don't

It's night and you're nervous so I say

I'll laugh at the lovers with you But I don't

I listen I feast I crack I batten

I miss you I lie I do I don't

Two women In a room left by someone else

Who knows what they're trying to say I don't

The emperor's harvest This boy I say
I don't think of him enough and I don't

Feast of razed Beit Lahiya orange grove
I say I'll share it but I don't

Feast of your voice in your body's absence
I say I'll rest there but I don't

Behold your upright citizen made faithless
I say I mean faithless but I don't

~24~

Petal of flame on a steel door
You could turn away If you touch it take care

A steel door between worlds One the emperor's
One unborn If you try to cross take care

Take your mask if it calms you Your fireproof coat
Then take them off Where I can see Take care

A cut on my lip in a place you know
When you reach for what will heal it take care

Who's waiting A cut girl A burning boy
Your dangerous cautioner A steel door Take care

~25~

for A

I must have missed the day this was discussed
Teach me then What is a person

This mask This way This face I've borrowed
from the old ones From you Is the owner a person

The way a stranger is not a stranger
Would I understand this if I were a person

The way this ruled island moves and whispers
and presses against me Does it think I'm a person

A palace Not a tent A hawk Not a perch
A message Not a messenger Is this a person

Who is that sitting across the table
A variation on Body & Soul or a person

The chastened lovers making way
for the ceremony of the chosen person

The individuality documents
I can't seem to keep on my person

To have and to hold the rain on the river
A glint of the unbroken braid A person

A spark in clothing When she comes in a dream
I can smell her So one of us must be a person

Come sit with your half-deaf union-rent comrade
Did you say misprision Or prison Or person

~26~

How had I grown so accustomed to moorings
Now your voice carries me from the slip to the sea

Dizzy untied Beneath and above
Again tonight Carry me The slip to the sea

~27~

You're sleeping alone and far tonight aren't you
Beside your flock Exquisite shepherd

The arch stronger than the lintel The arc
of your dreaming stronger than the arch Exquisite shepherd

If a gesture strays you gather it
With your hands Your voice Exquisite shepherd

When you come home will you break the fast
with dates and milk Exquisite shepherd

The crook and the rough blanket left on the grass
In the rock cleft For when you return Exquisite shepherd

Honey there In the old nest's ashes
The taste when you wake at home Exquisite shepherd

Whose mark was that on the grass beside you
Whose messages left in your hair Exquisite shepherd

~28~

In the booth of his tank Half young man Half machine
Saying the prayers for the harvest blessing

Branch of a date palm over the hatch
Unaccommodated night Blessing

Who were strangers once To shelter To weapons
Whose temple with a gun to it now Blessing

In the body of his tigress he crouches
to crush the enemy braziers Blessing

Hoshanah The stripped leaves will green but not yet
The willow will slake its thirst Blessing

He wanders armored and under orders
Sukkah of steel Victor's tabernacle Blessing

A stranger can hear his fathers weeping
His mothers calling him home Blessing

~29~

The emperor stripping the island with his teeth
The name in his mouth like a pit Manhattan

For you not the fruit but the ransom bit
Taste this to avoid another Manhattan

The man whose shirt smells of men not kissed
Pacing his choked many-masted Manhattan

The man whose body became a postmark
on a burning letter from Kabul to Manhattan

Old men sitting together in the evenings
playing dominoes In Shatila In Manhattan

Women spreading the Ghana Pentecost cloth
in the Dutch church across the strait from Manhattan

The woman's body washed by her mother
The mourning song from Najaf to Manhattan

Amsterdam for trade Columbus for force
Whose word is this Manhattan

If you like the emperor put your mark here
Let word of the new world go forth from Manhattan

Let the smell of death Do you remember
Let those it sickened testify from Manhattan

School but of weeping Law but of life
Davening and *salat* but of lovers In Manhattan

The neck of the island and the cuff made it fit
The emperor playing with the key marked Manhattan

Rebels in the plazas Death from the sky
Braziers in the rain In Gaza In Manhattan

The sound as the little hope bones are broken
Coffee Gin Laughter Bitter blue Manhattan

Trade and force The slave market at Wall and the river
left to its own free devices in Manhattan

The nation dancing at the charnel party
but not unhooded haunted Manhattan

One broken walker Spitting out the bit
and dreaming of fruit Not sleeping In Manhattan

~30~

Twitching in sleep Reaching for you
Foolish Faithful My left hand

Hearing winter's stripped moaning in the distance
Hiding in my pocket My left hand

Held up to ward off the glare of the searchlights
Guard marks at the wrist My left hand

Stumbler Slacker Slow at its lessons
Maimed listener My left hand

The off ox Hearing the whip orders dimly
Distracted by heart music My left hand

Stained mirror Fingertips smeared with guards' ink
and the newspapers' grief My left hand

Architect of a city that doesn't exist
Where your cheek rests against my left hand

Against your lips but not to hush you
and not those lips My left hand

Dear Mother my empty-sleeved grandfather wrote
I am trying this with my left hand

Dear besieged city wrote the girl born there
I write backwards Fleeing backwards With my left hand

Conducting the movement of silence for the street
made corpses and stones My left hand

City of peace But not here Not yet
A map on the palm of my left hand

Here's your gardener Planting garlic and hibiscus
at the edge of winter with my left hand

~31~

Terrace of olive Terrace of pear
The high city Refuge from summer heat Whose

Stone wall traces in a maple grove
Cornfield flecked with bone Whose

Terrace of mulberry Almond Lemon
Rifles on string slings for children Whose

I will break the nation in pieces
An island A village burning Whose

Terrace of pomegranate Nettle and mallow
A restricted road hacked in the dirt Whose

Salt cordgrass Minnows in winter The fish hawks
falling Called by the wrong name Whose

Sumac Chicory Mustard Mint
The tank turrets sweeping the market stalls Whose

The boys sitting at the feet of their fathers
To make a desolation Whose

Harvest of theft Dust to obscure it
Plunder to yield a richness Whose

Babylon many times demolished
The forbidden gestures buried there Whose

Attached to a ghost of a woman weeping
The phantom hand writing this Whose

~32~

The slanted light The winter coming
The leaves in drifts the color of honey

The men who believe the cure for shame
is murder Plotting in shops that sell honey

If you hear an airplane meet me in the cellar
The winter walls lined with August honey

After bees roll in the poppies' black dust
over fields of ordnance what's the taste of the honey

The winter hive in the rock cleft dust
Is this the presence or absence of honey

The sweep of your legs Your restless pacing
What's between Honor A borrowed lock Honey

Nectar to flight to spit and labor
The dance Life to death Interrupted by honey

Flecked with shrapnel and shirt threads of old children
Broken webs Weapon grease Still Honey

The soldier from the waist down made of steel
She who remembers him made of honey

The gulled harvesters breaking jars in the street
because they forget the taste of the honey

The one without it who comes at night
and naked and says the prayer for it Honey

~33~

Where the veiled woman escaped the crusaders
and hanged herself in the refugee camp Strange place

Kalashnikov fire from the minaret in the morning
Cannon fire answering Strange place

A soldier's letter Geese overhead
as the sun sets To see them in this strange place

If I ask will you mark where tenderness
persists on the map of this strange place

The treasure emptied so markets and feast days
may become drought and jackals This strange place

This body you've awakened to no purpose
What shall I do with it in this strange place

For the day cordite For night thyme and the moon
and a breath caught between in this strange place

~34~

When you ask in a dream if I'll ride with you
it's late and I'm barefoot but I say Certainly

When I lean to kiss you you start to say no
but the night interrupts to say Certainly

The flank of a mare running Dark rough sea
talking to the beach until dawn Certainly

With no saddle will the mare's back hold you
Hold me My hands at your waist Certainly

Two women Are those their masks or their faces
Moving through a dark salt place Certainly

~35~

Two chairs and a deck of cards Do you know
this dreamer's proverb *Paciencia y barajar*

As your hands disconcert Amalgamate
To shuffle To dance *Paciencia y barajar*

Temper *Métis* The winter wind mixing
the avenues' languages *Paciencia y barajar*

When she bucks all night in the stall Her flanks wet
and I whisper *Paciencia y barajar*

Two glasses of gin but mine smells like water
so I can smell you *Paciencia y barajar*

Your hand to your bare ankle when you're thinking
To see the cards' faces *Paciencia y barajar*

Your hand to the wrist of your tilting rider
Inviting and staying *Paciencia y barajar*

~36~

Cumin from eight thousand miles away
Amchur Lemon myrtle The emperor's plate

Malaysian pepper Meccan dates
Taste every nuance The emperor's plate

Between Amsterdam and Columbus it arrives
in the hands of a thin boy The emperor's plate

Tenderloin and a glass of Bordeaux
in my dream In your mouth The emperor's plate

The farmer's feast of drought and debt
in Rajasthan The emperor's plate

The lost farmer The lovers by candlelight
leaning over the emperor's plate

Partners in crime One in savor One in tears
and a ghost Sharing it The emperor's plate

~37~

Who is she That girl with gray in her hair
who holds your hands behind your back

The children lined up at the barricades
Their hands whitelashed behind their backs

A twelve-year-old girl in a twenty-year-old grave
in Río Negro Hands behind her back

The black bracelets we paid for A man in soft clothes
in Mosul Barefoot Hands behind his back

Salt balm but it's forbidden to go there
Come With our hands behind our backs

The prayer mat slick with sweat You're God's wish
Your hands clasped behind your back

A marble A blue mussel shell A penny
In one hand Which Behind your back

The Río Negro rifles called Galilee History
weeping with its hands behind its back

My daughter dancing my grandmother's sorrow songs
Feet free Hands behind her back

City of brick framing quarrels and dancing
City with the moon behind its back

Here's your acrobat Shoulders deft though aching
Taking you in my arms with my hands behind my back

~38~

Early dusk Rain Chestnut braziers
It's like that now in that place you mentioned

Casement windows The shallow balcony paved
with sycamore leaves in that place you mentioned

A white bed The Hotel Qui-êtes-vous
What's your name *Dis-moi* That place you mentioned

A tray of tea A little deprivation
Not easy to find in that place you mentioned

2 rue Secrète 2 rue de la Paix
Not on the maps of the place you mentioned

The Marais The lovers The boys of Drancy
lost and found in the little place The place you mentioned

Intersection of shofar and muezzin
and cathedral censer The place you mentioned

One dusk You're twenty-nine I'm twenty
and teaching you *n'est-ce pas* in that place you mentioned

Moules frites The heap of blue shells The vanished
taut salt coaxed open in that place you mentioned

One dusk November Two women teaching
no one's bed God's name in that place you mentioned

Dear S you wrote past midnight Your letter
found me waiting tomorrow in that place you mentioned

~39~

When they meet in the lion's den Jasmine and cedar
their bed Tell me *Sin dejar cosa*

When the shepherd and his family met
the planes near Mosul Tell me *Sin dejar cosa*

Narrow streets inhospitable to machines
of death A map of kitchens *Sin dejar cosa*

The brook of your mouth The walker's thirst
attended Waterbearer *Sin dejar cosa*

A water truck Four children A hundred sheep
The emperor's charnel list *Sin dejar cosa*

Your narrowness around my fingers Your lips
to my ear Tell me *Sin dejar cosa*

I want to see the pilot who killed
my children she said *Sin dejar cosa*

Your fear the binding around your breasts
All night loosening *Sin dejar cosa*

Before the soldiers he's heretic dreaming
her mouth What she said to him *Sin dejar cosa*

How I faltered before you found me and touched
the scar on my forehead *Sin dejar cosa*

How the friendly and enemy children will tell
the emperor's folly *Sin dejar cosa*

How you stripped me like the fall wind strips a tree
Wise Exigent Terrible *Sin dejar cosa*

Goodnight from your baffled auditor trying
to reckon what's missing *Sin dejar cosa*

~40~

Against my better judgment Whether
I can or no I go where you are

The fragrance where your neck meets your shoulder
A path I follow to find where you are

From when the sun finds the west river until
it touches the east I go where you are

Scraps of ripped itineraries Tinder
for the fires that keep breaking out where you are

If peace were found where we look for it
Or past honor Past custom Past shame Where you are

Don't come you say so I wait for sleep
to fill the sail and bring me where you are

Here's your night navigator lost
Letting the current find where you are

~41~

Dawn fanfare for the imperial city
Five helicopters in the eastern sky

A fire necklace you can't take off
Five helicopters in the eastern sky

The moon in the west with part of its cheek gone
Five helicopters in the eastern sky

The sound of a wound that doesn't heal
Five helicopters in the eastern sky

Whose subject Whose object Whose citizen watching
five helicopters in the eastern sky

~42~

He thought he would die there The emperor's seal
fixed In shame In the lion's den

His left eye night in Babylon His right
night in Jerusalem In the lion's den

Put your fear in the arms around my neck
and we'll dance to it In the lion's den

Your mouth the start of a long path walked slowly
In darkness To the lion's den

Not the burned village Not the emperor's pit
but inside Cave of breath The lion's den

Captive and initiate The angel's sweat
erasing his tablet In the lion's den

In charge of the province Acquainted with dreams
Then dissolved once inside the lion's den

A place he was taught was for thieves and traitors
What he found Who found him In the lion's den

Captive Your legs around my waist
My hands at your wrists In the lion's den

How at first he preferred the emperor's boulder
to the gate to life The lion's den

The tan ribs of the new guards rising and falling
under his cheek In the lion's den

If you close your eyes maybe you'll see me better
In the darkness In the lion's den

~43~

Your mother found me in a dream Not the one
whose body bore you but someone else

The thicket of rifles made spears of wheat
Was it you who touched them or someone else

Waiting in the short light The early dark
A man with a shovel Or you Or someone else

The body of a young man I thought I knew
but the newspaper said it was someone else

When I touch myself my face is wet
and I pretend it's someone else

How a voice can slip past the barricade
Who are you Weren't you looking for someone else

Will you she asked Her hands over mine
Not your mother Someone else

His cheeks just roughened His wasted days
Not your son Don't worry Someone else

As you turned As you lifted your face to me
Oh excuse me I thought you were someone else

Whirlwind with feet planted Upward bow
Is that you Destroyer Or someone else

Someone said Yes I will to your messenger
This gap where a voice is Or someone else

~44~

When you laugh I remember a cold brook washing
a gull on the bank in its blood Saying Stay

The way the salt wind would find me in winter
and press my lips like a brand and say Stay

A dream of an apricot orchard burning
The ashes plowed into dirt Stay

Dawn like a torch thrown in an alley
The color I'd make you if you let me stay

The tipped nick of moon like a scar on your shoulder
Show me Send the guards away Stay

Why look among the living for this one
Say it in my language Stay

The boy with the knife raised over his throat
What God said to his father Stay

A woman with a lamb on her shoulders
Under the emperor's avenues Stay

Catacomb but of lovers A marrow lamp
Someone crouched with paint in his mouth Stay

A wall of lions A wall of bulls
A ram running the way you do Stay

Breathing its own air A path to the world
makes it vanish A holy place You can't stay

On a curved wall Two ochre stallions
One biting the other's shoulder Stay

Two women Crouched in a dry cave Painting fissures
What you say as you leave them Stay

~45~

Wasn't that your cheek against mine last night
Gin Streetlight When somebody loves you Impossible

When you reach the broken paddock fence
the sign will say Impossible

The color God painted my eyes A cross
between storm and ewerstream Impossible

All your wrong lovers without certificates
Stamped across their foreheads Impossible

Dear Torch Received your kind invitation
Regret conflagration impossible

You must mean a phantom Your hand at her waist
Your ache at her absence Not mine Impossible

A holy place in the emperor's city
A peach in a stone Impossible

You the mask of a ram I the mask of a bull
Horn chips *Mischling* Torn doors Impossible

Dance without footprints Dance with no name
in a room with no lovers not touching Impossible

Your eyes One protecting your sleeping son's dreaming
One torchlit and trying to close Impossible

Dear Lion Here's a gazelle Hold her
in your teeth but no biting Yours Impossible

~46~

How she left the hearth for the winter beach
and took off her clothes to be able to breathe

In those first days How the jasmine on the sill
filmed with ash continued to breathe

If I say it as a command will you stay
My hands on your chest like a lion's paws Breathe

The little boat in the reeds that held him
and brought him to where he could learn to breathe

Harrowed land Brokenglass street
To take the dead flesh off the burn To breathe

Things I didn't think I'd have to learn
To temper hunger To wait years To breathe

Your fingers tearing open a letter
The way you make the things you touch breathe

His torn shirt Telling the storm Every veil
Take it Put your mouth on mine Let me breathe

A feast waiting for when you're past hunger
When you've forgotten Then you can breathe

Smoke of a village Smoke of grilled meat
The smoke you try not to remember Breathe

It's easy Like pulling a chain through your throat
Like a hacksaw's work Just relax Just breathe

Fire made of air Scald of sustenance
One substance This world's one fragrance Breathe

Did you smell apricot smoke last night It was me
Writing you a letter Listening to you breathe

~47~

You left a few souvenirs last night
Three bent feathers Marks on my hips Angel

My brother's wounds open again by morning
All night they're closed and blessed by an angel

With your thumb you wipe the lipstick from my neck
so no one will know you've visited Angel

Is it true you're wearing a uniform now
Are you part of the emperor's legion Angel

The tideline of your sweat on the sheet
Your shoulders' labor Night swimmer Angel

A note on the pillow *Un rompecabeza*
Artichoke Thistle One of each from your angel

Who whispers sedition Who takes your clothes
of stone and gives you flesh Angel

In the morning my hips are broken and the ash
on the windowsill has a new name Angel

The sounds in the dark as you break me Is this
how someone grown gets born Angel

How you dream the guards take you away
for the heresy of your tenderness Angel

In the braid of us hard to tell one from the other
In the dark Two women Part ash Part angel

~48~

An invitation to visit your own city
Will you recognize it after what's been done

First we scan your eyes Your fingertips
You've seen this play You know how it's done

From the neighborhood that was called Andalus
Where the emperor's dividing was done

The back of the rebellion broken
The wedding oranges spilled The uprising done

Now kerosene Hauled water Shit in the streets
Your escorts will teach you how it's done

The earth was made a *masjid* for me
when the time of the house made of gold was done

This from a far witness Petty underwriter
of slaughter Of undoing Of what was done

~49~

In the hall of the emperors swords are provided
so they may kill only each other By hand

In the hall of the ambassadors a lecture
on writing letters of surrender By hand

In the hall of the lions the hunted ones healing
The yarrow ointment applied by hand

In the hall of the myrtles a pond hedged with blossom
The shape of a star The shape of a hand

In the hall of the sisters at midnight two women
reading the future from each other's hands

In the hall of the bath Does that strange light come
from the candles The moon Or the lovers' hands

In the hall of the boat called Al Hamra Your voyager
searching the night's softness for you By hand

~50~

The gate of God taking off every disguise
Was it always this Paradise Babel

The taste of the dust of the broken towers
on the tongues of the lovers The feast of Babel

Confusion of tongues Counterpoint
of reeds in wind Tempered keys of Babel

A hundred and one ways to praise the place
your breasts meet your breathing ribs In Babel

Your tongue a rudder The water my days
How you navigate the currents of Babel

My ear against your chest all night
The guild of sleepless translators in Babel

When she can't say words what are your signs
Palm kiss for Breakfast Nod for Now Babel

Im eshkachech let your living cacophony
die into one clear note O Babel

The emperor's scattering Hoping the people
would not understand each other Babel

A boy with a rifle Praise to the day
this language is forgotten Even in Babel

The man in the copy shop typing Bengali
Speaking Spanish to Yiddish English in Babel

To cut the knot of complexity
To trade for one meaning the life of Babel

Here's your Manichean Teaching her one split tongue
polyglot So this letter will reach you In Babel

~51~

The book of the century I entered halfway
Page held to the light Watermark A grave

At the island's tip a backhoe touching bone
Burned village made a countinghouse made a grave

The place my father was born A map of it
folded in my mother's pocket A grave

The spring midnight my daughter was born
as the century bent to dig one more grave

My son surveying his inheritance
Wind passing over blossoms Then a grave

Your bare feet firm at the lip of the trench
How you took off my shirt that smelled of the grave

In my dream your fingertips at my temples Your lips
searching for me at the edge of a grave

~52~

Three orchid blossoms on a stem Then four
Beauty beyond use unfolding

When the wrapped children doze on the winter street
it's the dance of their lovers they watch unfolding

The letter you wrote in the middle of the night
In my mind Then my fingers Then my dreams unfolding

The firstmonth short light we were born in
The waning moon's study of darkness unfolding

Did you think I couldn't touch you from here
Whose tongue to your lips then Searching Unfolding

How you reached across the barricade
to teach my clenched fist unfolding

Here's your blossom scholar Beside the tight bud
of the night that will be hours unfolding

~53~

Where you keep the sweet in your grief
There At the edges of your mouth

Where the sea finds the island finally
Salt and sweet in the river's mouth

After the night stammerings who's the dentist
rebuilding the broken sentences in my mouth

The razed man listening to God
with one hand over his son's mouth

Little hearth concert Greenstick harp
A lion guarding it My daughter's mouth

Nourishment disguising a hook
The tuna's eager foolish mouth

When I wake up I'm holding your sweater
The taste of lemon and mint in my mouth

To drink the water and not the wine
To kiss your cheek and not your mouth

The white throat of the orchid blossom
sweeping up to the violet mouth

Lighthouse beam sweeping winter wave darkness
Marking the way to the harbor's mouth

Did you find the note I left on the branch
I watched blossom all night Held in your mouth

~54~

The storm skittering in the salt breeze
Just the taste of it on my lips for now

Time enough for the dance with the infinite
Kiss me the way we can for now

We've put jasmine petals in the blanks on their forms
Let the magistrates leave us alone for now

It's late so the guards keeping track of your travels
to my room forget You can stay for now

That which happened and that which will
Two stories I forget for now

Your lips on mine as you're laughing A letter
I save for later Marked For Now

The no night in which I will not touch you passing
Your dreamer leaving the dream of you For now

~55~

Passacaglia for your voice playing changes
on the four notes of dusk traffic again

On Columbus the man who lost someone asking
for change beside the stripped gingko again

If you tell me the words I'll speak to this thirst
and take its identity papers again

How even when they took the drums
he played with bare hands And dancing And again

The repeated ground Dusk washing in scarlet
the gray of the winter street again

Ostinato Stubborn reiteration
Not hunched walking with you not beside me again

Blues in the key of Where you been baby
Of Tell me slow Of Say it again

When she sings it once only half the house faints
So she has to smile and sing it again

The bridge between dusk and breakfast become
the back of your neck to your sacrum again

Between gray and black the avenue's blue
Sapphire for the lost man's keening again

Here's your dodger Running to slip a note
through the narrowness under your locked door again

~56~

The capital streets made cattle chutes
for the four horsemen of the coronation

Roses and crepe Commandos Consent
All arranged in the night for the coronation

The checkpoint faces wreathed in sable
and scarf masks for gas At the coronation

The children imitating the republic are more
beautiful than the republic at the coronation

The horses dressed The riders missing
A pageant of absence A coronation

As if it were not ours but his
Watching the screen of the coronation

At the edge a stenographer Listening for the monologue
gun salute's answer at the coronation

~57~

I can't see it but I can hear the current
moving the ice along the river

Your smell in the dark when I close my eyes
My dreaming the raft and your voice the river

The place the ocean finds to touch
what it is and isn't The mouth of the river

From the window over her bed you might glimpse it
A glint between winter buildings The river

The current flowing in both directions
Salt's long talk with sweet The river

Mud trough paved with dazzle The way the sun
sets cold fires the length of the river

Two women One shadow The skiff they share
moored not to land but to the river

~58~

What the painter found in every face
God's promiscuous note Human beauty

The filthy snow melting The afternoon light
torching wet pavements to open their beauty

What the stripped man owns His secret His freedom
from the bars of the guard's uniform His beauty

It's the song in her that radiates
into lion grace and appears as her beauty

In that room you swore never to visit again
In the mirror by the bed there Whose beauty

The blank pages of the book of the future
called Field Guide To War's Terrible Beauty

When you think your reasonable mouth is making
sober counsel it's making beauty

The lunatic lover alive called no name
but Mad After death called Who Uncovers Beauty

When she's found the solace of resignation
and the angel sends the incursion of beauty

In your curses Your slips Your appetite
In your touch beyond jurisprudence Beauty

She with no name yet dancing all night
with an arsonist Manacles undone With beauty

~59~

Is this why my hips ache in the morning
From dancing in circles all night with no one

Is this a kiss Your lips in a dream
Is this a prayer A whisper to no one

When the guard stops me by the river I show
my pass with its photograph of no one

Question Who will not meet you by the river
that doesn't exist Answer No one

A tour of the emperor's model city
City inhabited by no one

Hard on the heart Easy on shoe leather
Cheek to cheek tango all night with no one

Yours devoted to fabrications Writing
to a phantom who meets me by the river To no one

~60~

The forced forsythia wet on the counter
because the first vase she chose was broken

The stirring in the tight buds when winter's
seal on the storehouse of daylight is broken

The meal without you I eat with my fingers
The slick give when the shrimp shells are broken

I carry this watch because the face tells
the time although the hands are broken

The emperor's men who thought the rebellion
would stop if the children's arms were broken

For the emperor's windows hurled stones made
from the stone houses the emperor left broken

The emperor's squads of heroic women
who touch the stripped men and deliver them broken

In my pockets bits of unused tickets
Smelling of smoke Borrowed Blue Broken

How she scrabbled on the floor to assemble
the pieces of what my sons had broken

Forgive me my stranger Whose eyes I can't meet
For what's beyond healing now What's broken

Shall I stop with the dumb leaper in my chest
On and on Keeping bad time Faithful Broken

~61~

After the ebb tide Winter night
to dawn The rockweed frozen Then wet

In the book about hard a petal inscribed
with the secret aquifer history of wet

How the noon gray avenue puts on its beauty
when it's late Shiny black Light-laced Wet

When you found me I thought I'd mastered desiccation
When I found you your cheeks were wet

Lilit Night creature Your late letters stained
with smoke and wine Burn marks and wet

How you make my jeans and my wise right hand
and my ceremonial handkerchiefs wet

The woman spilled on the slaver's decking
The dress that is not her dress torn and wet

Exile prayer Take this filth from me
Home prayer Make me wet

How when he tore her the angel came
to bind her to life To make her wet

When I close my eyes you ransack my room
and leave the sheets and the history books wet

When you're open enough to forget the name given
by the mother who didn't know you When you're wet

When I pick it up my fingers see
you've left the harmonica's mouth wet

The print of your kiss on my jaw on the street
Yrs in the freshet and thirsty Yrs wet

~62~

How I wrap a cord around my dog's neck
to indicate he belongs to me

The emperor's guards make the cities dust
and then the sad mothers belong to me

How your left third finger catches the light
signaling You belong to me

If I put a flag in an island Salt green
wrapped in the bay It belongs to me

These hands my daughter will dream when I'm dead
Their gestures in hers Which belong to me

The memory of the plum at the end of winter
Among the ghosts that belong to me

Mud under the silk catkin willow Your voice
mud and silk Saying You belong to me

Two ears like the anther filaments of a blossom
Two used blue eyes that belong to me

Not by touch nor by law nor by custom
How is it then that you belong to me

This tongue borrowed from my ancestors If
I dance with it does it belong to me

This gin joint's proprietor's list Grief Song Shame
Your voice in a dream What belongs to me

~63~

The end of my dream of you smells like jasmine
The end of winter diesel soot and blue

Crimson on snow A cold painting of warm
Dawn's third movement After black After blue

Another invitation Leave my arms if you want to
This bed in my ear unslept in Leave it blue

Bend the notes of the winter sunlight
so they stay Rueful laugh in pieces Ache blue

How she holds the words missing from the letter
until the tips of her fingers are blue

Another rehearsal To see that evenin
sun go down Saffron Burned currant Blue

The words between your words I keep
The note between the notes that's blue

On the white avenue it's just a sad story
In the warmth of her throat alive Blue

How the stripped ones could hardly lift their heads
before the rebel invention of blue

Your mouth on my mouth to whisper No
Heap of shells after the feast Empty Blue

Here's your night porter carrying it in her face
Two letters with bad news Brimming Blue

~64~

The bridge between winter and spring
not made of steel but of melting

Not yet but here's the wet overture
The ice on the lilac branches melting

Salt Noon dazzle April The word
come in your mouth Agents of melting

One hand cataloguing solids The other
lost in the braided pathways of melting

Who's in charge of how you awaken me
The emperor or the angel of melting

The witness the guards broke and finished Packed in ice
His name remembered and told by the melting

The emperor's technicians of phosphorous
Diagrams of enemy children melting

I've brought something sweet that won't keep
Made for your mouth For now For melting

Your mouth A door between worlds where it's raining
Solvent of division A kind of melting

Two hands Whose Tangled in your hair
One in henna One in melting

Who's wrestling the angel's arduous blessing
Yrs dislocated Yrs slipping Yrs melting

~65~

On the shelf of the mailbox the guards have permitted
to stay The stripped stem of a rose

Before its time it presses from the canes
Not June in the curbside garden Not a rose

What shall I bring you Ink instead of ache
The story of a rose instead of a rose

In the salt thicket Not last year's but the new
but not yet In the entryway A rose

You could call it purposeless Or wet silk
Or lush path your mama named blind Or rose

Between Columbus and Amsterdam
June night quarrel between diesel and rose

The way those who fled the burned villages
saw messages in the way the smoke rose

The man asked to show his documents
who handed the guard a lit match and a rose

Cubes fitted with chains in the tropical prison
In each a book of suras and a rose

How he had to remember his name again
every time the sun rose

There Not there Your gardener sees it
in April A ripped jacket June A rose

~66~

I'm used to the emperor's bitterness
I can't find the sweet place unless you make me

This face that is not my face I may
look made but when you touch me you make me

Make the oak say blossom The stripped say swell
The avenue pavement say river Make me

This shirt I can't take off The one
the nights without you gathered to make me

The new day The sweet place Tomorrow
whispering from tonight's last light Make me

Kissing you without authorization
If you want me to stop you'll have to make me

The ruined city Or is it a woman
interrupting your sleep to say Now To say Make me

~67~

I dreamed a gold room behind my eyes
and then I could stay Then I could see you

The man on his knees covering his face
against radiance Weeping Let me see you

To swim from the smoke wreck until I can't
lift my arms Then the fragrance of land To see you

The way I look into the cherry branches
the moon opens And away To see you

Whose hand wrote you on my eyes
so when I close them I can see you

If your wrists ache let me undo the buttons
of your uniform Let me see you

How I study the oyster's beauty without
the silver fork Eyes closed to see you

Cinders Nearsightedness Distance Tears
Which makes it most difficult to see you

Songs Jokes Caresses that leave no trace
What I would give tonight to see you

When I tried on the uniform you gave me
my tears dried but I couldn't see you

Here's a hand you know Making these marks on a page
to find you tonight with scratched music To see you

~68~

The barbarian girl who sells herbs and tinctures
Whose name is also Beloved And Ruth

E and B who couldn't stop loving her
Who said her strange name in the night Ruth

In Bethlehem she who stutters the language
Whose passbook says Special Registration and Ruth

Whose mother was not her mother Whose place
she carried in her own mouth Ruth

A word to mean Bent To Gather The Leavings
Severed Auctioned Faithful Ruth

How in the night she mocked and kissed
the streets of the place she came from Ruth

The mother of the new way a foreigner
A mouth full of enemy languages Ruth

Who makes music from outside the covenant
Whose name is David And also Ruth

Who looked on a strange woman and could not
be kept from her Also known as Ruth

The bound altar dove who calls the strange fields
she sees flying free Home Ruth

Yours outside jurisdiction No relation
Sitting with a near stranger tonight With Ruth

~69~

How I lie with my back pressed to conquering
to watch the profligate moon pass over

The bread of affliction Of haste and hatred
That the night it seems will not end may pass over

How I walk garbling in my prayers
the names of those whose bones I pass over

They take you in the morning Or the others Blood
on the doorposts to say Not here Pass over

When you kneel and lean with your breasts to my mouth
and the days without milk and almonds pass over

The cup set aside should the one who would say
Next year in peace decide to pass over

Your infidel in the broken city
waits for your fragrance to pass over

~70~

My hand by my daughter's hand The rough
apple branch and the delicate blossom

The city lights tangled in the branches Here's how
she dances This world of fire and blossom

At the tips of the maple branches in the snow
Invisible flickers of red blossom

Did you think I had forgotten you
The whisper of the peregrine blossom

Hunched in its jacket to last the winter
Who says Now to start the blossom

At the intersection In the crossroads gutter
Wet soot Lipstick cigarette butts One white blossom

The curved moon passes through the forsythia
and litters the west rooftops with blossom

When she missed the snow he tried to console her
with a walk through an almond orchard in blossom

Last night you told me No with your shirt
left on the bed and your arms full of blossom

To forget you let me eradicate night
and women singing and harbors and blossom

Your implacable researcher keeps missing it
Noting ache Dreaming blossom

~71~

When you ask for my documents I show you
the torn uniforms of my brothers

That light from the pit is Joseph dreaming
the dream that will save the lives of his brothers

Their arms around each other's necks
A man and a woman who are brothers

The boy who used to live there passing
what were doors Looking for his brothers

Where the bakery was The barbershop
Broken glass and a litter of brothers

What is it you're looking for when you break her
in pieces A woman A city My brothers

How we cut ourselves the way we were cut
and made the wounds kiss so we would be brothers

In the work of love we failed each other
In the work of killing we became brothers

Before the emperor sends them to die
for nothing he calls them his sons and his brothers

Thou shalt exalt and gull and spend
and crush and tear and waste them My brothers

She forgets the codes of the uniforms
A sister Searching smoke streets for her brothers

~72~

The salt thicket where there may be roses
I put my hand nearby Then in

Spring and its crowbar of light prying open
my packing case and barreling in

I dreamed I kept a cart on the street
to sell bandages that let sunlight in

I heard you tapping at the window last night
but when I beckoned you wouldn't come in

How your hips make mine ache when you bend to look
for what Which corner is what you lost in

First outside Ask me Say my name
Then near Then at the wet edges Then in

My name is also The Children's Compass
and one more I'll tell you if you let me in

~73~

The wool at your neck when you turned up your collar
The silk at your throat when we were walking

The ordnance attended by expert mechanics
and flown The soldiers and the citizens walking

Not your kiss then Not your face soft from sleep
and the years I've watched gather there But walking

Where she saw the little boat tied in the rushes
She with scarred ankles and a child walking

I've lost my grandmother's ring and the room
where you touch me But not tears And not walking

The castoff one in borrowed garments
talking all night to the city by walking

Praise cold water to rinse the salt from her face
after dreams of a gold room Yrs waking Yrs walking

~74~

How have I come to this strange place
Whose words in whose mouth Wearing whose body

Almoneda Almendra Auction and almond
arguing all night over my body

Did she risk or court the emperor's sentence
when she went to bury her brother's body

To suggest this cluster of bombs be converted
to a field of poppies I address which body

How I recognize someone I met in an orchard
at night in the smell at your neck In your body

Before A girl in an alleyway
arguing with her mother After A body

He who addresses the soul and sprinkles
lime on the extrajudicial body

Yes I will touch you everywhere
Except where you live Except in your body

How I carried her wrapped in graveclothes until
you said her name Why And woke her This body

The one who cleans the city of the people
The one who divides the soul from the body

Posted outside the emperor's prisons
The rock of justice Where is the body

Who lived Who wore it as long as she could
and then one dusk took it off Her body

Called Trash Waste Dust Shamed for its hungers
The faithful persistence of life in a body

To eat To drink To love To sleep
To work To die The truth of a body

A map of a mined garden Two blue pools
Two stripped wings Two roses One gold room This body

This ache without end Is this your lesson
To teach what it means to live in a body

The rain's writing letters your slow one can't read
but they smell like a river remembering your body

~75~

The wildfire that threatens the houses made embers
Made ashes and scattered Death to death

The feast we'll have when my mouth has forgotten
this ache for yours To celebrate death

The Levite's concubine's hands on the threshold
What makes a sanctuary of death

The emperor's proclamation It's sweet
and fitting Feed it your children Viva death

Now she can walk in the village accepted
She who's learned the customs of death

The pines gapped and burned by acid smoke
Dawn mist passing among them Passing death

The whisper that is not a whisper Teach
my body deafness to yours Teach me death

The river of fire of being alive
Dam it Divert it Dilute it with death

Slaughtered beginnings Winter's leavings made May
Which face are you wearing tonight oh death

Beneath the pageant of liberty
another hidden pageant Of death

Here's your collaborator Practicing treason
to sanctuary To forgetting To death

~76~

How she slept on cardboard outside a bank
and dreamed of an egg in a cup in a room

In this reel the torn child laughs in her sleep
and the tangle of rebar becomes a room

I've forgotten the constables' instructions
The letters of transit All I know is this room

How the soldiers walked through the walls to make
stripped ruin where there had been a room

Behind your lips a harbor where it's raining
and a candle and a key to a borrowed room

The skyline a Braille text of late lights Each
a sign of someone awake in a room

Behind the buttons of your shirt an old city
A feast and a fire in an old stone room

On the last day they tried the attic just before
the guards came but there wasn't room

A necklace of prisons at the nation's throat
How to breathe through the smell coming up from that room

Erased from the maps you can find it still
This covert behind my eyes This room

It's cold Come share your sailor's watchcoat
A hearth A room where there is no room

~77~

The children no one is hunting dancing
in drifts of cherry petals with no shoes

If you want to know where I slept last night
don't believe my documents Ask my shoes

Before you cross this threshold take off
your keys Your grindstone grist Your shoes

Before I come you touch your hair
and sit by the window to take off your shoes

The old woman who lost someone Who went
wading and forgot to take off her shoes

To forget you I try to teach my skin silence
My tongue commandments My bare feet shoes

The burning to crimson The quenching steam
The pinned hammering To give a horse shoes

For each citizen A teacher A roof
A doctor A song Milk and honey and shoes

How I close my eyes touching a woman not
you and put on my traveling shoes

How they carry me through the days without you
My good soldiers My counterrevolutionary shoes

Walker you call me in a dream Your hand
at my chest to stop me Your bare feet on my shoes

~78~

Folded in the pocket of a gambler leaving
the barred window The number of my days

Fingertip test Will this cut
the thread of your voice from the cloth of my days

What is this tree you've planted Crowning
Blossoming Dying in the courtyard of my days

What I put in your hands My body made of words
Used moonlight My wet handkerchief My days

It's finished Thief Stranger I will give you nothing
but all my nights All my days

~79~

What she wears as she wearies of life Black boots
dusted with pollen and bits of grass

Among the ruins of September
Shards of morning Rats Rain Grass

What the prophet wore in the desert to dream
Hunger and thirst and a girdle of grass

In the soldiers' sandals so they could keep walking
What the mare's strength is made of Grass

How she lasted the winter but found herself
undone by the return of the grass

The darkness that made us a private room
as you acquainted my hips with the grass

On the first day without you to dream of your mouth
On the sixth day of sand to dream of grass

For the emperor's thirst seven prostrate cities
For mine your mouth For the bull's dawn grass

Monday at nine His grindstone His work
He and his camerado Shirts stained with grass

The low egret at dusk reading the night
from the tufts and cowlicks of the salt grass

Our grandchildren's plans for the emperor's triumphs
Lamentation Repentance Stone dust Grass

The mark in the sand where she slept beside him
This is his brook edged with banks of grass

Your empty-pocketed walker here sending
instead of a letter thirteen slips of grass

~80~

How her footsteps crossing blurred the borders
Wet Without papers Wilderness Barbarian

The rock of Tarik Dark lighthouse
for a raft and an unaccommodated barbarian

The whirlwind at the world's western edge
to mark the beginning of the barbarian

The promontories from Algeciras
Almost touching One nosotros One barbarian

If you go there If I follow you If
they forget which of us to call barbarian

A ship's hold fitted with chains A bomb
of infinite radiance Not barbarian

In the barbed hamlet In the vilayet
Ask her body questions and she'll answer in barbarian

From the archipelago of camps Incessant
prayers and songs and curses in barbarian

Wind over the trench graves gathering
every lost nuance of barbarian

How the clean men learn to make bodies dead
then gather in secret to play barbarian

Make him jabber Foul his holy things
Call him One Forsaken in barbarian

Reduced to the radiance of a body
But the days to come made of this Of barbarian

Here's your lover of Babel In the quarrel conducted
in Scripture Empiric Your tongue And Barbarian

~81~

Do I know your taste and the ache in your voice
from a night beach in another world

In a borrowed bed one afternoon It was raining
But no You must mean another world

The last light playing the grackles' blacks
in this or is it another world

How he fell with a red map on his chest
A page from an atlas of another world

The child fresh from it trying to remember
how this tune goes in another world

At the checkpoint each suspect holding two passports
One for this and one for another world

Received your last invitation The one
to a locked door to another world

How she found him pressed to the wall of a tunnel
and whispered a message from another world

How they named the cut places for their fathers
to forget they'd been touched by another world

How she lives in a camp with her grandchildren
and carries the key to another world

Sometimes in her weariness a fragrance
The harbors and cooksmokes of another world

Glass dimming the street din when you said
where you'd like to touch me In another world

Your traveler's shirt has two fragrances
One from this and one from another world

~82~

When they left the garden for the world
was it a fall or a radiance

On your hair On the shoulders of your jacket
On your lips The rain's dispersed radiance

Shining from the emperor's crest
Pirated scraps of the people's radiance

A shell packed with arrows Whose dream was this
Whose fury Whose hunger Whose wound Whose radiance

The kidnapped olive her grandfather knew
as a boy The torn roots' radiance

A uniform the color of a desert A forest
A city To disguise his radiance

The storks' last prayers from the minaret nests
The still leaves of the courtyard fig Evening's radiance

Can you find me without using your eyes
With your hands In the night's radiance

What touches me from across the room
Your soul in its reckless radiance

A seed planted in the mouth of a girl
Now a maple Blasted Persistent A radiance

From my grandmother in Damascus via theft
and caress to Manhattan Unbroken radiance

Will you take the tongue of my belt from its bindings
Behind it a gold room A radiance

Do you see the red in the eastern sky
You're shielding your eyes From sleep From radiance

~83~

Sun spilling over the banks of Canal Street
Yesterday's rain stored in a cistern

All the lips the lush cosmopolitan
June rain will touch on the way to the cistern

Enough for a flock and a kitchen The river
uninterrupted Not a dam but a cistern

Protector of dates where there is no spring
The tools to cut it from granite A cistern

Where the blood hesitates before being sent
on its lawless errands The heart A cistern

How Joseph's dreams touched the walls of his prison
and left wet breath on the stones of the cistern

Two pearls from the necklace at the desert's breast
One a prison One a cistern

Breast of rock Water furnace
Your cupped hands for my sadness A cistern

A torn uniform on a boy's torn chest
A flag's shadow flying from the shadow of a cistern

To sustain the lemon The tray of mint
The lamb in the strafed dooryard A cistern

Two women forgetting the curfew The room
where they meet Where the rain runs in A cistern

~84~

If not for my lips My tongue My throat
The fragrance then of holy wine

The last May dusk waiting night for you
Sluicing the sidewalks with holy wine

Whose touch required to make the water
of bane and oblivion holy wine

Walking among the desolate sleepers
on Amsterdam Handing out holy wine

Will you keep calling it out of its name
because it's as close as your own Holy wine

From the burst black jackets The flesh transformed
The vineyard in winter feigning death Holy wine

No magistrate No judge No priest
to confirm its bitter and sweet Holy wine

The new vessel To let it breathe in its brilliance
Your mouth the decanter of holy wine

Do you know that bar on 69th Street
that serves not forgetting but holy wine

The grass under a maple in the darkness
The bread of courage and holy wine

Salud Here's your host and guest still
on her feet To life Via holy wine

~85~

How he'd kept it a word of love until
they made him say it in hatred Yes

To extinguish her To take her village
Her *abaya* Her face Her tongue Her yes

Though dim with sorrow Compassed by archers
Do you still belong to me Yes

When the angel asks and the broken woman
closes her eyes as a way to say yes

Did I dream it again or did your mouth
spend last night teaching mine a new language Yes

In her tongue Where the questioners couldn't find it
Are you now or have you ever been Yes

How you make my hips argue all night
between No I will not admit you and Yes

The way the trees speak different languages
in the months of No and the months of Yes

I dreamed I asked Will you walk with me
and you locked the door before you said yes

Four notes from your fingertips at midnight
No Yes No Yes

The stranger's face is the mother's here
and the lovers are strangers dancing Yes

~86~

If not the presence as darkness comes
then the taste of the absence of the beloved

The dust that was stone that was three rooms
in a house in a city she called beloved

Did he know who it was he tried to kill
A boy Maimed Murderous Beloved

Tell me all her sweet names for you
Glittering rill *Compañera* Beloved

When you didn't come What did you mean
when you said you'd lost your way beloved

Shall I call you stranger Or song not quite
forgotten Or shorn collaborator Or beloved

Will you pull the blinds so the sycamores
will forget we were here together beloved

How they made her kiss the checkpoint dirt
and call the border watchtowers beloved

The ruin the ruined guards bring to the nations
the emperor calls Mine and Beloved

Bless them In place of my lips and my hands
the words I use to touch you Beloved

I'm drawing the face you hide in my sleep
Whispering from behind the veil Beloved

~87~

Before the ploughshare turning up bone
Before the dance made dominion A sail

How he took down the mast of the stolen skiff
and hid drifting north wrapped in a sail

My grandfather's tools A settler's square
Green plank The patroon's patent A sail

The clanging of the halyards in the harbor
as you pass at night Implying a sail

Keel pressed to kelson inside Oar to lock
Arched hull planking to ribs Wind to sail

On the winter jackstand sandpaper and sweat
and the trace of the dance of what's free Of a sail

The thrum of the kelson in the soles of your feet
The invisible current read by a sail

A salt room pulling against the mooring
toward walking on water Toward a sail

The head of the mast fit in the cleft kelson
Then the whipped halyard Then the sail

To move close-hauled Closer Almost with the wind
With the trembling in the throat of a sail

Here's your lover of the fragrance of land
trying to sound the waters To sail

~88~

Your lips on mine not weary Not faint
Your tongue a spring to open this fever

Among the gifts of my ancestors
The braid of life Rape Pillage Fever

The watchfires lit at my body's gates
so you will be able to find me Via fever

In its blur I tell you everything
In the tongue-loosening swelter In this fever

The last time I asked the night
the address of peace the answer was fever

My scorched shirt on the floor by the bed
afterwards Souvenir of fever

Here's your scholar of scalding At the meetingplace
between cool knowing current and fever

~89~

The vase of tower fragments and his mother's
last dress made ashes the wind blows loose

How the rain reaches into the winter ground
and warms and turns the grasses loose

Walk on your knees says the guard to his father
Give me a name and I'll turn you loose

The harbormaster's hands in the morning
on the knots the night tides tried to pull loose

The peony petals pressed in round bud
then unfolding Your shirt's pink Then falling loose

How the years found what she held so tightly
and took it Prying her fingers loose

Left in the tree he passed every day
A man The tatters of his clothes flapping loose

The smallness of the barbarians' airplanes
after the emperor's airplanes let loose

How he sat coughing shards of his nation's hatred
How she wanted to keep him and he said Turn me loose

The meadow paddock by the intransigent
sea broken open and the horses run loose

She's remembering your way with her bindings
Yrs bridled How you tighten How you cut them loose

~90~

To the creed of don't touch me and I will not
touch you stranger I am faithful

With curb and reproof Here Wear this disguise
The garments with which I was taught to be faithful

How she stood for three days outside the prison
in her helplessness Witness Faithful

Blues in F as the sun goes down and our bodies'
knowledge and solace but no We are faithful

Making you moan until dawn lover only
here A vocation to which I am faithful

To protect you from the authorities Those
at the door and those in your eyes Ancient Faithful

The razed city The men in a pit The women
divided and taken Pageant of the faithful

Breaking curfew to sleep by the olive tree
who spoke in a woman's voice Foolish Faithful

To the razed city's persistence To your lips
kissed so long they tell the truth Faithful

How he weeps on Ishmael's banishing day
Those to whom he cannot help but keep faithful

Yrs between the ruled streets and the night journey
The emperor's and the angel's Faithful

~91~

I'm going where the emperor's cigarettes
burn boys Will you accompany me

Could I find the grove where the path of ashes
turns if someone would accompany me

What Hagar banished said to the man
she knew Who will accompany me

At the smell of the burning city I lose
my way without you Accompany me

How he stands by the sweating drummer and plays
the searching song called Accompany Me

Through the desert cities without the barbed wire
beloved of emperors Accompany me

What the angel said by the tree of life
she couldn't see yet Accompany me

How can I walk where the ground burns my feet
without your voice to accompany me

How you put your hand over this hand not yours
What you make my hips say Accompany me

Noah's dove after the end of the world
The ark's other name Accompany Me

Here's your asker with an imperative
Through the days left Accompany me

~92~

Assignment Find the shirt that will keep
my nipples from rising at the sound of your voice

What God said to David My son taught war
let me teach you to sing in a lover's voice

How he laid his bound son on the pyre because
he thought he heard his father's voice

Only your hands and your mouth bring stones
in the emperor's square Touch me with your voice

Slack to stiff Rigid to softened Chill
to melt Anarchic alchemist Your voice

How she wraps the burned man she cannot touch
in the balm and fury of a woman's voice

Here's your parched accomplice at the day's edge
listening for the night's gravel brook For your voice

~93~

How the guards preserve his life and foul
his body in order to take his soul

The vizier's cross for the master sergeant
Honored harrier of the enemy soul

Is this what's rising over the east rooftops
taking off her old clothes and mine Someone's soul

If not this what are you touching then
Inside me all night If not my soul

I see her smoking a cigarette on the terrace
Touching death with her lips and her fingers Your soul

The looks on the faces of the people gathered
at the salt island scaffold for the auction of her soul

Which is the translation and which
the original tongue The body The soul

The uprising your hand makes The heat and ache
The eloquent stammer of the body The soul

A kitchen for lovers and a woman singing
Why haven't you seen it Body and Soul

Not sure what to do with her outlawed hands
Hesitating in the doorway Whose soul

You've made me forget my name tonight
touching my body aka my soul

~94~

The dungeon in Ghana where the women were kept
The ceiling the floor of a church Hallelujah

Call it Babylon City of the body's joy
Let the smoke of it rise forever Hallelujah

How they dance on the grave of the woman who took off
the veil of her captivity Hallelujah

Your hands and what they make me say
A word for that sweet rent heresy Hallelujah

When you leave the house of your mother and father
for a stranger who knows your name Hallelujah

The hands of the holy men fixing the torches
of shame at the body's gates Hallelujah

In the word for the god the old word for the moon
who takes off her clothes and dances Hallelujah

His tears when he looked on the strangers consumed
instead of his maimed rejoicing Hallelujah

The arcs of ripe mulberry crushed on the pavement
Our bed of nettles and clover Hallelujah

Amalek From Moab and Sidon And the Hittites
whose daughter made the psalmist moan Hallelujah

How in their armor they found the fountain
not of youth but of life And mistook it Hallelujah

When your hands ache from trying to hold the bridle
and when you let her run Hallelujah

Here's your faithful one looking for it still
A holy place A peach in a stone Hallelujah

~95~

Take my hands before they forget
the dances they used to know will you

The newspaper's grief says you never will
but maybe you missed that part Will you

How he hides from the village guarding her
to stand close enough to whisper Will you

Fool to moon as she takes her gold clothes off
Take mine while you're at it will you

What the angel asked via harrow and salt
and no name in the street Will you

What he says when his son visits the prison
Tell your mother I love her will you

The torn girl wearing the cloak that makes her
invisible Take it Carry it will you

The hellbent searching song he plays
through the night until morning Translation Will you

I've lost the map to the orchard A place
you know night wanderer Take me there will you

When I make the mistake of recognizing
you Stranger Forgive me Will you

She's writing it on the last piece of paper
When you open it's blank but her voice says Will you

~96~

The shod men who smelled of a dead land's ghost
What they made of the men they found barefoot

To do what you want with his soul take his costumes
His chestplate and cheekplates and greaves Make him barefoot

New rule for the takers of land
Leave your machines and walk it barefoot

Permitted to pass Those with no names
or papers Those scorned Those without Those barefoot

The common strangeness of shoes arguing
all night with the local strangeness of barefoot

Asked to the emperor's banquet you come
with your lover's mouth Cursing and blessing Barefoot

Do you think your wakeful one can't see you there
watching and waiting Redhanded Barefoot

~97~

How he walked the hills where the people had died
under his protection as a kind of healing

The rain's way with the shards of September
Touching and bearing away Healing

The girl who had no choice but to walk
on the broken place as it was healing

Under the bandage of darkness The night
the wound's plummet tilts toward healing

She learns to tell them apart by their fruits
The pain of waste and the pain of healing

My transgressor My dove My undefiled
What the fathers called filth and the lovers called healing

She's rewriting the arson warrants tonight
Yrs blessed in the fire Yrs annealed Yrs healing

~98~

My left hand in my hair My right
holding you and writing this poem

This bent message This sheaf of notes
From the whirling night this piece This poem

Hiding and watching the host of young men
and touching himself and making his poem

Whose messenger from the commotion
Whose footfalls just before Whose poem

This scattering This archipelago
scored by straits of silence This poem

How they knew who he was by what they found
in his coat pocket after A witness A poem

In my ninety-eighth dream you and I were sailing
not in a harbor but in a poem

How it burned from the binding of its fascicle
A lightning bolt disguised as a poem

What did not protect her but made a place
where her soul could learn to live A poem

From the margins After When the emperor's edicts
are ashes A song stripped of music A poem

Under my fingers the wetness of this
commission This way you touch me This poem

~99~

Who found the dress she left on the sand
in the darkness in which she walked out of life

How she touched the grafted cherries
to forget what her father taught her was life

How I watch the moon cross like a letter between us
The vigil that has become my life

If what you think is life is a dream
and what you think a dream is life

The boy soldier's glory and the veteran's shame
Which did they treasure His death or his life

The moment before he begs them to take it
The last time he begs for his life

How the rains bring ruin and relief
and leave in their wake devastation and life

Rolled in the arms of a roughneck gambler
who laughs like you do In the arms of life

The night journey to whose temple To the bed
that smells not of smoke but of lovers Of life

When she asked the winter scrabble camp tree
its name who answered Life Life

Leave my mouth then but first set a seal there
Of balm for affliction Of joy Of life

Can't you taste it yourself In that bold devoted
asking and knowing My outlaw Life

What is this thread with which you've bound me
to an orchard in a storm To life

~100~

Under the green if you see with your mind
Maple blossom answering winter with red

In the bull's eyes last Not the matador
but the curve of the cresting wave of red

The color of touch me and touch-me-not
A cherry Held in your wise teeth Red

The lion pinned in whose embrace
Her eyes half closed Her mouth smeared red

My eyes after another night like this Wine
on your lips I can't see North and south Red

How they steal past the guards holding the bridles
and ride until the sky is red

Here's one more scratch song From a blackbird Dark flight
interrupted by flashes of red

~101~

Leaving the feast of your mouth in a dream
for the ache of the waking sidewalk today

The woman who slept with her cheek on the pavement
waking with the sun in her eyes today

Repeating itself in whose fever dream
Whose sidewalk market made charnel today

Where are you my comrade Making whose grief
laugh Salt and walking my comrades today

Not dusk Not the night where we rode until
not dawn Not riding Not we Today

Your face in my dreams like the water the wind
touches and moves Touched Here's today

One last note From this hand you opened
In the palm a kiss Yours Yesterday Today

Notes

Re the letter to Shahid: See *Call Me Ishmael Tonight: A Book of Ghazals* (Norton 2003), and *Ravishing Disunities: Real Ghazals in English* (Wesleyan 2000), Agha Shahid Ali (1949-2001).

radif: a ghazal's repeated refrain.

makhta: a ghazal's final couplet, which the poet 'signs,' with an image or a pseudonym or a name.

Elizabeth T. Gray, Jr., on the ghazals of Ḥáfiz: "And everything seems ambiguous: is the poet talking to the one he loves? Or is he reproaching a patron? Or is this a nugget of wisdom aimed at the disciple who seeks union with God? If the poet is talking to or for his beloved, is the beloved a man or a woman? Is it actually the poet talking?"

Martha Zweig: "...the ghazal's couplets are quixotic, each takes another tilt at the poem's material; the speaker flirts, beguiled into the next and the next couplet by the will-o'-the-wisp glimmer of the last."

Agha Shahid Ali: "The ghazal is made up of couplets, each autonomous, thematically and emotionally complete in itself: One couplet may be comic, another tragic, another romantic, another religious, another political...One should at any time be able to pluck a couplet like a stone from a necklace, and it should continue to shine in that vivid isolation, though it would have a different lustre among and with the other stones."

Ibid.: "What defines the ghazal is a constant longing."

Re the epigraphs: The *Song of Songs* verse is from the King James translation. *Cántico Espiritual*, San Juan de la Cruz, translated by Elaine Valby as "Soul-Song," stanza 27:

"There he gave me his chest.
There he taught me the sweetest science.
And I gave him the whole

of me, withholding nothing.
There I promised to be his lover."

The Koran verse is from the JM Rodwell translation. Thanks to Leticia López for finding it.

#6 See Billie Holiday, "All the Way."

#8 *Za'tar*: a mix of spices with thyme and sumac evident, maybe also including sesame seeds, salt, paprika, hyssop, olive wood, marjoram, or oregano. *Lebneh*: creamy cheese made from strained yogurt. *Ka'ik*: a round bread. *Yellah*: Let's go. *Ma'asalaama*: Goodbye. *Shukran*: Thank you.

#11 "Those the guards touch strapped in ice and plastic" refers to to Manadel al-Jamadi, killed at Abu Ghraib prison in Iraq in November 2003 after being beaten by members of the Navy SEALS and turned over to CIA interrogators. See "CIA Is Likely to Avoid Charges in Most Prisoner Deaths," *New York Times*, October 23, 2005.

#15 *Zukkar*: Sugar in Arabic. *Azúcar*: Sugar in Spanish. *Sabor y saber*: Savor and know.

#17 *Je voudrais te dire pero imposible*: I would like to tell you but impossible.

#19 Assam: teagrowing region in northeast India. Kericho: teagrowing region in Kenya.

#20 Re the sixth couplet, see Herman Melville on boys from Vermont and New Hampshire in 19th century New Bedford, waiting for their first whaling voyage to begin:

"Now when a country dandy like this takes it into his head to make a distinguished reputation,
and joins the great whale-fishery, you should see the comical things he does upon reaching the
seaport. In bespeaking his sea-outfit, he orders bell-buttons to his waistcoats; straps to his
canvas trowsers. Ah, poor Hay-Seed! how bitterly will burst those straps in the first howling gale,
when thou art driven, straps, buttons, and all, down the throat of the tempest."

Moby Dick

#29: *Davening*: Jewish prayer. *Salat*: Muslim prayer.

#31 The high city is Ramallah. The fish hawks are near New Bedford, Massachusetts: osprey, whom the white settlers didn't recognize and called 'buzzards,' hence Buzzards Bay. 'Babylon many times demolished' is from Michael Hamburger's translation of "Questions from A Worker Who Reads," Bertolt Brecht.

#35 *Paciencia y barajar*: from *Don Quixote*, 'Patience and shuffle the cards." *Métis*: half-caste, cross-bred, mongrel, hybrid.

#36 *Amchur*: mango powder. Rajasthan: spicegrowing region in northwest India, in which nearly 2,000 farmers committed suicide between 1999 and 2002:

"Our system of food security is being destroyed in the name of economic growth and economic liberalization, and people don't have enough food to eat. Our farmers are being ravished by seed companies, being pushed into debt, and committing suicide...

"The way out of this violent cycle is to deepen democracy—to bring decisions that directly affect people's lives as close as possible to where people are and to where they can take responsibility...

"What we have now is a regime of absolute rights in the hands of corporations with zero responsibility for the environmental and social devastation and the political instabilities they are creating. If we want to reactivate and rejuvenate democracy, we have to bring back the economic content." Vandana Shiva, 2003

#37 In March 1982, over 177 women and children were killed by soldiers and their auxiliaries in the village of Río Negro in Guatemala. In January 1994, the remains of at least 143 victims were exhumed from three mass graves. The people were killed because they resisted eviction and resettlement in the wake of the building of the Chixoy Hydroelectric Dam, funded by the World Bank. The soldiers carried Israeli rifles called Galil, which means Galilee.

#38 The Marais district has been a Jewish neighborhood of Paris since the 13th century. In Yiddish it's sometimes been called the Pletzl, the little place. At 6 rue des Hospitalières-St-Gervais there's a Jewish boys' school, from which during the war 165 boys were deported to Drancy and from there to Auschwitz.

Qui-êtes-vous: Who are you, formal, or plural. *Dis-moi*: Tell me, familiar. The addresses translated would be #2 Secret Street, #2 Street of Peace. *Moules frites*: mussels with fries.

#39 *Sin dejar cosa*: from stanza 27, *Cántico Espiritual*, via Elaine Valby "withholding nothing": literally, without leaving out a thing. See also "The Secret War on Iraq," John Pilger, *The Daily Mirror*, December 18, 2002.

#42 See *The Book of Daniel.*

#43 Re 'upward bow,' aka 'urdhva dhanurasana,' see Vanda Scaravelli, *Awakening the Spine*: "We could compare this movement to a whirlwind that, after having sucked and turned the water violently downwards into an eddy vortex at tremendous speed, then lifts the massive conglomeration of water high up into the air, collecting it in a single column and rejecting it down into the sea once more."

" '...There is the image of the spiral movement which represents the "tornado,"...a curled power that created the world and moves in alternating motions of advance and retreat.' "

#44

Now upon the first day of the week, very early in the morning, they came unto the sepulchre, bringing the
spices which they had prepared, and certain others with them.
And they found the stone rolled away from the sepulchre.
And they entered in, and found not the body of the Lord Jesus.

And it came to pass, as they were much perplexed thereabout, behold, two men stood by them in shining garments:
And as they were afraid, and bowed down their faces to the earth, they said unto them, Why seek ye the living
among the dead?

Luke 24: 1-5

Re Lascaux, via www.metmuseum.org: "The painted walls of the interconnected series of caves in Lascaux in southwestern France are among the most impressive artistic creations of Paleolithic humans. Although there is one human image, most of the paintings depict animals found in the surrounding landscape, such as horses, bison, mammoth, ibex, aurochs, deer, and felines. No vegetation or illustration of the environment is portrayed around the animals, who are represented in profile and often standing in an alert and energetic stance. Their vitality is achieved by the broad, rhythmic outlines around areas of soft color...In the absence of natural light, these works could only have been created with the aid of torches and stone lamps filled with animal fat.

"...No brushes have been found, so in all probability the broad black outlines were applied using mats of moss or hair, or even with chunks of raw color. The surfaces appear to have been covered by paint blown directly from the mouth or through a tube; color-stained, hollowed-out bones have been found in the caves."

#45 *Mischling*: half-caste, cross-bred, mongrel, hybrid.

#46 See *The New York Times*, June 14, 2004, Randy Kennedy, "Journals of 2 Ex-Slaves Draw Vivid Portraits," on the narratives of John Washington and Wallace Turnage: "Mr. Turnage's story tells much more of the brutality of slavery, because most of his years of bondage were spent as a field hand in Alabama. He writes of near-crippling lashings of female slaves and describes four unsuccessful attempts to escape, some of them followed by severe beatings, before he finally succeeded in 1864 after hiding in a swamp for a week.

"While hiding, he often slept in an unused Confederate lookout perch. One morning, he writes, as if he were witnessing a miracle, he saw the tide bring something in.

" 'Now when I got down there I seen a little boat very small indeed though the tide was going out,' he says. 'It stood like it was held by an invisible hand; so I got in the little boat and it held me.' "

#47 *Un rompecabeza*: a puzzle, literally 'a break-head.'

#48. The city is Fallujah. "The earth was made a *masjid* for me": attributed to Mohammad by Jabir bin Abdullah. A *masjid* is a mosque.

#49 The halls are and are not in the Alhambra. 'Al Hamra' means 'the red one.'

#50 *Im eshkachech*: If I forget you. See Psalm 137: "If I forget thee, O Jerusalem, let my right hand forget her cunning."

#55 *Passacaglia*: A Baroque musical form based on continuous variations. Also a dance. Probably from the Spanish *pase*, to walk or pass, and *calle*, street. *Ostinato*: the repeated ground theme of a passacaglia, literally 'stubborn.'

#56 Re the fourth couplet: "The children imitating the cormorants/are even more beautiful/than the cormorants." Kobayashi Issa, 1763-1827. His name means "a cup of tea."

#58 See *The New York Times*, January 28, 2005, Michael Kimmelman, "Rembrandt's Late Religious Portraits: Humanity With Flaws Forgiven."

#68 See Julia Kristeva, "The Chosen People and the Choice of Foreignness," in *Strangers To Ourselves*, translated by Leon S. Roudiez: "If David is *also* Ruth, if the sovereign is *also* a Moabite, peace of mind will then never be his lot, but a constant quest for welcoming and going beyond the other in oneself." E and B are Elimelech and Boaz.

#74 See *The New York Times*, February 22, 2004, Carlotta Gall, "Risking Death, 2 Afghan Women Collected and Detonated U.S. Cluster Bombs in 2001."

Re "The rock of justice": "Sir William Blackstone, who wrote his famous Commentaries on the Laws of England in the 18th Century, recorded the first use of habeas corpus in 1305. But other writs with the same effect were used in the 12th Century, so it appears to have preceded Magna Carta in 1215.

"Its original use was more straightforward - a writ to bring a prisoner into court to testify in a pending trial. But what began as a weapon for the king and the courts became - as the political climate changed - protection for the individual against arbitrary detention by the state.

"It is thought to have been common law by the time of Magna Carta, which says in Article 39: 'No freeman shall be taken or imprisoned or disseised or exiled or in any way destroyed, nor will we go upon him nor will we send upon him except upon the lawful judgement of his peers or the law of the land.'" (BBC News, "A brief history of habeas corpus," March 9, 2005)

#75 Re the Levite's concubine, see Judges 19:27.

#80 Re "the rock of Tarik": Tarik ibn Ziyad was the Berber leader of the Muslim invaders of eighth-century Spain. Jebel-al-Tarik, Tarik's mountain, is also known as Gibraltar.

#84 See "A Case of You," Joni Mitchell, *Both Sides Now*, 2000.

#85 *abaya*: A long loose garment, Muslim modest dress.

#87 Re the third couplet: "The earliest ancestor in America was Jacob Janse Gardenier...born between 1615-1620 in the Netherlands. He was a carpenter or millwright and was under an apprenticeship when he came to America...Jacob returned to Holland in 1642 and found a position doing carpenter work in the new colony. He later returned to America in 1642 on the ship *de Houttyn*. Once Jacob was back in America he became quite the businessman owning at one time land on the North side of what today is known as Wall Street, from William to Pearl. He purchased the land for 1,000 pieces of green plank. Jacob became a land and mill owner near Kinderhook, NY where he and many of his descendants lived. He also owned a sloop which made many trips on the Hudson River." From *The Gardenier/Gordinier Family*, Hollace Carey Gordinier, Jr., 1990.

A halyard is a rope for raising or lowering a sail; a keel is the spine of a boat on the outside of the hull, a kelson the corresponding structure on the inside. A whipped rope is one with its loose ends bound to prevent unraveling.

And:
"I believe in you my soul, the other I am must not abase itself to you,
And you must not be abased to the other.

Loaf with me on the grass, loose the stop from your throat,
Not words, not music or rhyme I want, not custom or lecture, not even the best,
Only the lull I like, the hum of your valved voice.

I mind how once we lay such a transparent summer morning,

How you settled your head athwart my hips and gently turn'd over upon me,
And parted the shirt from my bosom-bone, and plunged your tongue to my bare-stript heart,
And reach'd till you felt my beard, and reach'd till you held my feet.

Swiftly arose and spread around me the peace and knowledge that pass all the argument of the earth,
And I know that the hand of God is the promise of my own,
And I know that the spirit of God is the brother of my own,
And that all the men ever born are also my brothers, and the women my sisters and lovers,
And that a kelson of the creation is love..."

Walt Whitman, "Song of Myself"

#89 "...I just remembered his face, a bright, blunt, handsome face, and his weariness, which he wore like his skin, and the way he said *ro-aad* for road, and his telling me how the tatters of clothes from a lynched body hung, flapping, in the tree for days, and how he had to pass that tree every day. Medgar. Gone."

James Baldwin, "No Name in the Street"

And: "Medgar Evers was returning from a glum strategy session...His own white dress shirt made a perfect target for the killer waiting in a fragrant stand of honeysuckle across the street. One loud crack sent a bullet from a .30-'06 deer rifle exploding through his back, out the front of his chest, and on through his living room window to spend itself against a kitchen refrigerator...The victim said nothing until neighbors and police hoisted the mess of him onto a mattress and into a station wagon. 'Sit me up!' he ordered sharply, then, 'Turn me loose!' These were the last words of Medgar Evers, who was pronounced dead an hour later." Taylor Branch, *Parting the Waters*

#91 See *The New York Times,* June 13, 2005, Neil A. Lewis, "Some Held at Guantánamo Are Minors, Lawyers Say": "One lawyer said that his client, a Saudi of Chadian descent, was not yet 15 when he was captured and has told him that he was beaten regularly in his early days at Guantánamo, hanged by his wrists for hours at a time and that an interrogator pressed a burning cigarette into his arm."

#94 See Psalm 104:

" The glory of the Lord shall endure for ever: the Lord shall rejoice in his works.
He looketh on the earth, and it trembleth: he toucheth the hills, and they smoke.
I will sing unto the Lord as long as I live: I will sing praise to my God while I have my being.
My meditation of him shall be sweet: I will be glad in the Lord.
Let the sinners be consumed out of the earth, and let the wicked be no more. Bless thou the Lord, O my soul. Praise ye the Lord." [In Hebrew: 'Hallelujah.']

Re the dungeon in Ghana, thanks to Emily Gropp for describing it to me.

The Moabites and Sidonians and Hittites are peoples of ancient Palestine described in the Bible as enemies of the Hebrews. Bathsheba was a Hittite, first lover and then wife of David and mother of Solomon.

Re Amalek, see Numbers 13:29: "Amalek dwells in the land of the South: and the Hittite, and the Jebusite, and the Amorite, dwell in the hill country; and the Canaanite dwells by the sea, and along by the side of the Jordan."

And: "And so Amalek became Haman (who actually was an Amalekite), who became the Romans, who became the Crusaders, who became Chmielnicki, who became Petlura, who became Hitler, who became Arafat...a number of things need to be said about Amalek, and about the Amalekization of the present enemy. For a start, the prescription of an eternal war with Amalek was a prescription for the Jews to be cruel. Here is Rashi's brutal gloss, in the eleventh century in France, on the commandment to 'blot out the remembrance': 'Every man and every woman, every babe and every suckling, every ox and every sheep. The memory of Amalek cannot be said to survive even in an animal, such that someone could say, "This animal once belonged to an Amalekite."' This extreme of heartlessness was responsible for the most chilling sentence uttered by an Israelite in the Bible: 'What meaneth then this bleating of the sheep in mine ears, and the lowing of the oxen which I hear?' That was what Samuel furiously demanded to know of the poignantly human Saul, the king who could not bring himself to slaughter his enemy completely."

Leon Wieseltier, *The New Republic*, May 27, 2002

#97 “I sleep, but my heart waketh: it is the voice of my beloved that knocketh, saying, Open to me, my sister, my love, my dove, my undefiled: for my head is filled with dew, and my locks with the drops of the night.”
Song of Songs 5:2

#98 “Now one is removed from the commotion, removed into the most silent, speechless heavenly kingdom--removed even from language, which the commotion once laboriously created to be its messenger and handmaiden, and which, since the beginning of its existence, desires eternally the one impossible thing: to set its foot on the neck of the commotion and to become all poem--truth, purity, poem.” Martin Buber, *Ecstatic Confessions*

(Gracias, compañera.)